Anonymous

Memorial Addresses on the Life and Character of John

Covode

Anonymous

Memorial Addresses on the Life and Character of John Covode

ISBN/EAN: 9783744660785

Printed in Europe, USA, Canada, Australia, Japan

Cover: Foto ©ninafisch / pixelio.de

More available books at **www.hansebooks.com**

John Covode

MEMORIAL ADDRESSES

ON THE

LIFE AND CHARACTER

OF

JOHN COVODE,

A REPRESENTATIVE FROM PENNSYLVANIA,

DELIVERED IN THE

SENATE AND HOUSE OF REPRESENTATIVES,

FEBRUARY 9 AND 10, 1871.

WASHINGTON:
GOVERNMENT PRINTING OFFICE.
1871.

REMARKS OF MR. KELLEY, OF PENNSYLVANIA.

Mr. SPEAKER: We have again been painfully reminded that there is an appointed time to man on earth, and that he is consumed, and vanisheth away as the cloud. When on Friday, the 6th of January, he left Washington for a brief visit to Philadelphia and Harrisburg, few of us appeared to have a firmer hold on life or the more assured promise of a green and comfortable old age than my late colleague, Hon. John Covode. Descending from ancestors on either side whose lives had been prolonged beyond the allotted period, endowed with a robust and muscular frame, and having enjoyed singular immunity from disease, he was happy in the thought that at the expiration of this Congress he was to return to private life and devote his energies to the promotion of several enterprises in which his interests and feelings were engaged. But it was not so appointed. He was not to return to his place in this hall; and the execution of his cherished purposes was to be confided to other hands.

From Philadelphia he went with his younger sons to West Chester, Pennsylvania, to replace them in the excellent academy in which they had been receiving those educational advantages of which untoward circumstances had deprived their father. Accompanied by his wife he proceeded to Harrisburg on the 10th of January. He was in the enjoyment of his usual vigorous health, and passed the evening in cheerful intercourse with friends assembled at its capital from the several quarters of his native State. Expecting to take the early morning train, he retired early and slept, free from apprehension of the dread summoner. About three o'clock he was awaked by a severe pain about the heart. What wife and friends and medical skill could do for his relief was done; but in less than two brief hours the strong man feebly gasped the dread words, "I am dying," and passed beyond the sphere of temporal trials or triumphs.

A distinguished citizen of Massachusetts, in the course of an elaborate article entitled "The Government and the Railroad Corporations," in the last number of the North American Review, in characterizing the people of Pennsylvania, says:

"They are not marked by intelligence. They are, in fact, dull, uninteresting, very slow, and very persevering. These are qualities, however, which they hold in common with the ancient Romans. And they possess also, in a marked degree, one other characteristic of that classic race, the power of organization, and through it of command. They have always decided our presidential elections; they have always, in their dull, heavy fashion, regulated our economical policy; their iron-masters have, in truth, proved iron masters indeed, when viewed by other localities through the medium of the protective system by them imposed. Not open to argument, not receptive of ideas, not given to flashes of brilliant execution, this State none the less knows well what it wants, and knows equally well how to organize to secure it."

The author of this paragraph would probably have found little to commend in the character and career of Mr. Covode, who was born in the mountainous wilds of Western Pennsylvania many years before that State had provided common schools for its children, and whose childhood and youth were passed in toil on a farm and in a woolen mill. He had not studied the writings of Kant, Fichte, or Hegel, or even made himself familiar with those of Carlyle or Emerson. But, ignorant as he may have been of the doctrine of intuitive perceptions and the body of transcendental philosophy, he had, without these aids, attained such a knowledge of the uses of material nature, and the springs that animate, impel, or restrain men, as made him the welcome and trusted counselor, when maturing their grandest projects, of men far more learned, brilliant, and distinguished than himself. His letters contain no quotations from classic authors, but are replete with evidence of his sagacity, insight into the motives of men, and masculine and matured judgment.

Mr. Covode was born in Westmoreland County, Pennsylvania, on the 17th of March, 1808. That his parentage was humble will be inferred from the fact that his grandfather, Garrett Covode, a native of Holland, was when a child kidnapped in the streets of Amsterdam by a sea-captain, who brought him to Philadelphia and under then existing laws sold him into bondage as a "redemptioner," in which condition he was held for some years after coming to manhood, and was subsequently employed as a domestic servant in the household of General Washington. He died in 1826 at the advanced age of ninety-four years. The mother of Mr. Covode was a Quaker, and it is among the traditions of her family that two of her ancestors, together with a person named Wood, prepared and published a protest against the decision of William Penn recognizing the legality of African slavery. This protest is said to have been the first anti-slavery manifesto published in this country.

The first public office filled by Mr. Covode was that of justice of the peace "for Ligonier and Fairfield Townships," to which he was appointed by Governor Wolf before he was twenty-four years of age. Then, and in this humble office, it was that his neighbors bestowed upon him the *sobriquet* of honest John Covode. His office, to which angry litigants were summoned, was in truth a court of conciliation, in which, regardless of the emoluments of office, the judge found his duty and pleasure in adjusting by compromise disputed claims between neighbors and soothing their exasperation.

In 1845 he was nominated by the Whig conferees of the counties of Somerset and Westmorland as the candidate of that party for State Senator. The district was largely Democratic and he was defeated, although he received several hundred more votes than any other candidate on the State or local ticket of his party. At the next senatorial election he was again nominated, and such was his personal popularity that though both counties gave large Democratic majorities for the general ticket, he came within fifty votes of election. In 1854 he was nominated for Congress by the Whigs of the nineteenth district, consisting of Westmoreland, Indiana, and Armstrong Counties. His competitor had been returned at the preceding election by a large majority, but Mr. Covode led him 2,757 votes, and was returned. This was the Thirty-fourth Congress, and he was re-elected to the Thirty-fifth, Thirty-sixth, and Thirty-seventh.

On the 5th of March, 1860, he introduced a resolution providing for a committee of five members of the House "for the purpose of investigating whether the President of the United States or any other officer of the Government has, by money, patronage, or other improper means, sought to influence the action of Congress, or any committees thereof, for or against the passage of any law appertaining to the rights of any State or Territory," &c.

Few who were engaged in the political struggles of those days will forget the industry, energy, and ability with which Mr. Covode conducted the investigation ordered by this resolution, or the influence his elaborate report had upon the public mind. The report was a thorough exposure of the corrupt appliances by which the Kansas-Nebraska legislation had been secured, and was soon in the hands of every Republican speaker or writer in the country.

Mr. Covode was twice married, and had three sons by his first marriage, all of whom he gave to the country upon the breaking out of the war. George, the eldest, rose by gradual and well-won promotion to the rank of colonel, and was killed, while leading his regiment, at the battle of St. Mary's Church, in 1864. The youngest, Jacob, pined for more than eighteen months in the loathsome and pestilential pen provided for Union prisoners at Andersonville. He still lives, a broken and prematurely old man. Mr. Covode's industry and enterprise had meanwhile secured him an ample competence, and with his sons he was ready to devote this, too, to his country; and while bankers and capitalists were doubting the propriety of investing in the war loan about to be issued, the telegraph informed the people that John Covode had apprised the Secretary of the Treasury of his purpose to take $50,000 of the forthcoming bonds.

He was a member of the Joint Committee on the Conduct of the War. To the labors of this committee he devoted himself with untiring zeal until the 4th of March, 1863, when, having declined a nomination, he retired from Congress. Availing himself of the knowledge Mr. Covode had thus acquired, and of his quick perception of the motives of men, President Johnson requested him to make a tour of observation through the unreconstructed States and report his conclusions and the general facts upon which they were based. But, observing the change that had taken place in the views and purposes of the President, he soon returned and submitted a report, which was never made public, though the House called upon the President for a copy thereof.

Mr. Covode having refused to be a candidate, the district was represented by a Democrat, Hon. John L. Dawson, in the Thirty-eighth and Thirty-ninth Congresses. Yielding to the demands of his party, he however accepted a nomination for the Fortieth and was returned by a handsome majority, and was, after a contest by Hon. Henry D. Foster, also awarded a seat in the Forty-first Congress. His influence was not confined to his county or congressional district. It was felt throughout the State, not only in politics, but in all measures projected for the development of its boundless material resources. Having been appointed to the position in 1869, and conducted the campaign that resulted in the re-election of Governor Geary, he was at the time of his death chairman of the Republican State central committee.

In comparatively early manhood he became the owner of the woolen mill in which he had been employed when a boy. He watched with interest our progress in the manufacture of textiles, and labored to promote their diversification and perfection. But his mill did not offer an adequate field for his activity. He took a zealous part in promoting the construction of internal improvements by which the seaboard should be connected with the then opening West, and on the completion of the Pennsylvania Canal engaged largely in the business of transportation. He was also a liberal and energetic promoter of the construction of the Pennsylvania Central Railroad. On the completion of this road to Lockport, where he lived and superintended his mill, he concentrated his stock upon the western sections of the canal and engaged in forwarding to and from Pittsburg the rapidly increasing freight moved by the railroad. About this time he also organized the Westmoreland Coal Company, which has developed the immense deposits of gas coal that underlie in such affluence his native hills.   By this operation he added to the wealth of every farmer in the county, for the army of stalwart men now earning liberal wages by mining and handling this coal is so numerous that it gives them a steady home market, not only for the cereals, but the minor productions of the farm which will not bear extended transportation.

Mr. Speaker, what I have said is sufficient to show that Mr. Covode was a man of power and a useful citizen.   He had long been a member of the Methodist Episcopal Church, was faithful in all the relations of life, and his story may be read with profit by the youth of the country.   Born subject to those "twin jailers of the daring heart, low birth and iron fortune," and receiving the benefits of but the smallest opportunities for early culture, he mastered fortune, commanded the confidence of his neighbors and fellow-citizens, and secured for his name an honorable place in his country's history, and, by originating and promoting beneficent enterprises, wrote it enduringly on the hills and in the homes of his native county.   He left a wife and seven children to mourn his sudden death.   The results of his provident care surround them, and their sorrow is alleviated by the confident assurance that he who was so fondly devoted to them has entered upon the rewards that are earned by a well-spent life.

Mr. Speaker, I submit the following resolutions:

Resolved, That the House has heard with deep regret of the death of Honorable John Covode, a member of this House from the State of Pennsylvania.

Resolved, That, as a testimony of respect to the memory of the deceased, the officers and members of this House will wear the usual badge of mourning for the space of thirty days.

Resolved, That a copy of these resolutions be transmitted to the family of the deceased by the Clerk.

Resolved, That the House, as a further mark of respect to the deceased, do now adjourn.

REMARKS OF MR. BANKS, OF MASSACHUSETTS.

It is a common event, Mr. Speaker, that interrupts the regular course of legislative business, and calls upon us to reflect upon the loss we have sustained by the death of the late honorable member of the House from Pennsylvania, to consider our relations to each other and to the great Author of our being. No occurrence is more frequent. There is not a day, not an hour, scarcely a minute passes over us that some recruit or veteran in the great army of life does not drop by our side or within our sight.

It is not violence or crime, disease or excess alone, that gives death its victory. It has other means of conquest than the shot and shock of battle, the murderous affray, the indulgence of passion, or the storm and tempest in the physical world. Though human passions were extinct and men as guileless as the flowers of the field, still the carnage would go on. Death would still reap its regular and prolific harvest. There are seeds as well as instruments of death. They are sown everywhere—in hills, in drills, and broadcast. No clime so rugged, no soil so barren, that it will not bear this fruit. That which falls even by the wayside or upon stony ground is not lost.

This is the harvest that never fails. No class of men escapes. Our predecessors in these classic Halls have been swept away by battalions. The paths of granite and marble that lead to the Capitol have been worn away by the unceasing and heavy tread of anxious and solemn men that from every part of the Union have come here to meditate upon the necessities and to labor for the improvement and preservation of the Government. Where are they now? Death has spared but few. Of a score and a half of Congresses, perhaps more, even now, in the infancy of our Government, not one living voice is heard, no representative remains. The best, the bravest, the noblest of our land, all are gone. Madison, Monroe, Adams, Polk, Clay, Benton, Webster, Calhoun, Macon, Douglas, Broderick, Giddings, Davis, Wilmot, Stevens, Burlingame, are but types of the hosts that have preceded us to the only haven of rest for wearied, exhausted, betrayed human nature.

It is a common event, therefore, that summons us to suspend
deliberation upon the affairs of life, that we may consider for a moment
those of eternity. That which makes it seem particular with us is
that it stole upon us without our knowledge; swept from our side the
stalwart form of active and vigorous life upon which we relied for
help in committee, in session, and in society; broke up the quorum
of associates and friends, and left us stunned, standing in helpless
silence, knowing only what shadows we are, and what shadows we
pursue. Like time, the angel of death hides its wings as it ap-
proaches. It is when they are upon us and cover us that we comprehend the depth of that shadowless valley through which it takes
its flight. How difficult it is to comprehend, in this full blaze of
light and life, that the broad-shouldered, stalwart man who stood
beside us, his voice still ringing in our ears, unceasing in his activity,
doing no wrong, seeking only the good of others, should, even while
we turned to look upon him, disappear from our sight forever, and
his spirit by translation pass to another world!

The death of Mr. Covode reminds me how much we depend upon
others for the selection and acquaintance with our most intimate
associates. I knew him chiefly through my late lamented friend,
Mr. Burlingame. He was the earliest among many active and
sagacious men of the Thirty-fourth Congress to analyze his character
and accord due honor to the separate elements of which it was composed.

Mr. Burlingame was a harmonizer. It was his ambition to bring
those who should act together, to understand and know each other.
No man was ever endowed with more of this divine power. He appeared to feel instinctively not merely the presence of good or evil
spirits, but to measure with unerring justice the exact degree with
which innocent and baneful qualities were mixed in human character.
He looked upon the world with the eye of childhood, but he judged
it with almost more than mortal wisdom. Without effort and without
resistance he allowed its varied characters to be photographed upon
his mind; and thus he read, as by an unseen light, the secret natures
of men by whom he was surrounded and with whom he was associ-

ated. He knew all qualities certainly with a most learned spirit. It was this purpose and this power which gave him in speech, and still more in social intercourse, the great influence which he wielded here, and enabled him in another sphere to bring together unknown and hostile sections of the world with mutual satisfaction and advantage.

Mr. Burlingame was naturally and at once drawn into confidential and friendly relations with Mr. Covode, who, in a different way and upon a different class of persons, exercised the same important and beneficent influence. I shall never forget the delight with which Mr. Burlingame first spoke to me of having found in his new friend a kindred spirit. It is strange that men so unlike in condition, in habit, and in cultivation should be so drawn together; but it is the one common touch of nature makes the whole world kin. No two persons exercised a higher or purer influence in the Congress which brought them together, and their mutual esteem and friendship ended only with their lives. It would be impossible for me to pronounce a higher eulogium upon the character of the late member of the House than to repeat what I have so often heard fall from the eloquent lips of our common friend; and I am sure no estimate of character could be more highly prized by his family or friends, or by the members of the House around me, than a favorable judgment formed under such circumstances and considerately expressed by the distinguished man to whom I have referred.

The peculiar and prominent characteristics of Mr. Covode were his simplicity, sincerity, and earnestness. His convictions were clear and strong. He was necessarily a partisan, because he adhered to his convictions and those who supported them; but he was an honest and generous partisan. With the best opportunities to judge during the most excited period of our recent political history, I never observed in him the slightest tinge of malignity, of selfishness, or envy. There is no character of the heated period of which I speak that I recall with more unmixed satisfaction or higher respect.

There is no better illustration of the power of good sense, honest purposes, and earnest devotion, unaccompanied by the advantages of scholarship, than that which his career exhibits. He was, as his

distinguished and eloquent colleague has said, an uneducated man;
but there are elements of power more important in the management
of human affairs than polite learning or scholastic education.

> " Knowledge and wisdom, far from being one,
>   Have ofttimes no connection. Knowledge dwells
>   In heads replete with thoughts of other men;
>   Wisdom in minds attentive to their own.
>   Knowledge, a rude, unprofitable mass,
>   The mere material with which wisdom builds,
>   Till smoothed and squared and fitted in its place,
>   Doth but incumber where it seems to enrich."

Mr. Covode had this wisdom. There were few among us who
had a larger share of influence in public affairs when he gave them
his attention, or could better impress his convictions upon the masses
of the people.

Without any of the graces of oratory, his speeches, short, senten-
tious, apposite, and replete with enthusiasm, never failed to produce
the effect which is both the purpose and result of true eloquence—
that of challenging attention and working conviction. His addresses
to popular assemblies were of this character; practical, enriched with
copious illustrations, pertinent to his argument, never above the
comprehension of his auditors, and never failing to carry conviction
to those whom he addressed. The political campaigns that followed
the presidential election of 1856, especially those which brought in
review the incidents of the distinguished administration of Mr.
Buchanan, gave signal evidence of his success and power.

There was a religious tinge in all his thoughts and actions not
unlike that attributed to Huguenots and Puritans, but which gave
him a somewhat different character. Though a stern partisan he did
not counsel extreme measures. A generous policy, enforced with
unity and vigor, represented his theory of wise political action.
When party necessities carried men beyond this he was a cool,
reluctant, if not halting supporter. It has been said, and I believe
with entire truth, that it was due to the direct action and influence of
Mr. Covode that Mr. President Lincoln was led, against the advice

of some of the most prominent of his supporters, to issue the order directing the immediate and unreserved exchange of prisoners of war during the latter period of the great rebellion. If this be true, no man can present a more honorable claim to the respect of the people, without reference to political opinions or partisan relations. This view of his character is strengthened by the fact that he never failed or faltered in support of those measures which were deemed necessary to protect and preserve the Government and to secure and perpetuate the liberties of all its people.

Though we lament his death, we cannot be unconscious that our loss is his gain. He exchanges one life for another. It is not annihilation, but ascension that he has attained. He will suffer no longer the disappointment which attends the expectation and the effort to make the world virtuous by statute legislation or despotic administration. He has passed to a higher wisdom and holier existence. He is done with the vanities of life, with its

> " Reveries so airy, with the toil
> Of dropping buckets into empty wells,
> And growing old in drawing nothing up."

The death of Mr. Covode is one of the many events which impart to all men an unaccustomed feeling of insecurity. Death produces death and calamity begets calamity. The terrible afflictions which within a few years have passed over the face of the earth, crushing empires and states as well as individuals, more than ever should lead us to recognize our dependence upon the beneficent will of the Creator of the world. It should teach us as well that permanent success follows only justice and truth; that there is but one law— the law of God—to which the world should be subjected; and that—

> "One Spirit, His
> Who bore the platted thorns with bleeding brows,
> Rules universal nature."

REMARKS OF MR. MERCUR, OF PENNSYLVANIA.

Mr. Speaker: I feel unwilling to suffer this occasion to pass without briefly adding my tribute to a departed friend.

John Covode's life was a striking illustration of the success which will crown the works of an earnest and laborious man. Deprived in his youth of the advantages of a liberal education, he felt the greater need of literally working his way to enable him to rise in eminence and to fortune. This he determined to do. Strong physical powers, clear practical mind, and indomitable will, all united in impelling him onward and upward. His was a mind that was not contented to occupy any uncertain position. No so-called "conservative" doctrines ever deterred him from pursuing the right, as he saw it. Sprung from liberty-loving ancestors, he retained all their notions of freedom, but grafted thereon a greater love, begotten by the spirit of this progressive age. His opinions once carefully formed, no timidity characterized their expression. He followed his convictions to their logical consequences. Men who united their political fortunes with his felt a confidence that he would continue as he began, and not turn aside and leave them without a standard-bearer to lead them.

Neither his accumulated wealth nor his prominent position in the eye of the nation ever estranged him from his early and less fortunate associates. Dwelling in the small but beautiful and retired valley of the Ligonier, in his native county of Westmoreland, he never appeared to desire a home elsewhere. The rugged hills which surrounded his residence seemed to give strength to his judgment and freedom to his speech.

When, in obedience to a resolution of this House, I stood beside his coffin, and hundreds of his neighbors and friends passed before it, I saw unmistakable evidence of the esteem and affection which they had borne toward him. With pride they had viewed his elevation and success in life. They shared in his reputation. His honor was their honor. No jealousies had separated them. He had ever returned to them the same social, kind, and unassuming friend. His was a nature to mourn with them when they mourned, and to rejoice with them when they rejoiced. A true type of our republican institutions, he never for a moment lost sight of that great cardinal doctrine that ours is "a Government of the people, for the people, and by the people."

Suddenly stricken down in the midst of his active life, this House has lost one of its most faithful members, the nation one of its watchful legislators, the State of Pennsylvania one of its best known and most enterprising citizens, and his family a kind and indulgent husband and father.

REMARKS OF MR. NIBLACK, OF INDIANA.

Mr. SPEAKER: I feel that I ought not to allow this occasion to pass without adding a few words.

Very few persons on this side of the House, outside of his own State, have perhaps known the deceased as long and as well as I have. When, in December, 1857, I first entered this House as one of its members, I found him here as one of the Representatives from Pennsylvania, and I soon afterward made his acquaintance. He was then, I think, serving on his second term. He was one of the very few I then met who are now members of either of the two Houses of Congress. Although neither of us have been since continuously members of this body, yet it has so happened that this makes the fourth Congress, I believe, in which we have served simultaneously.

Soon after thus first meeting him we were thrown together on some tedious and rather important committee work, which required almost daily meetings for many weeks, and which brought us into frequent and unreserved personal association. That association ripened into a rather intimate personal acquaintance, and from that time to the day of our last meeting we always met rather as old neighbors and familiar friends are accustomed to meet than as new-made acquaintances, representing different and distant States. And however much we may have differed in our political views and party associations, nothing of a personally unpleasant character ever occurred between us.

I have seldom since met him that he did not have some cheerful word to impart or something quaint and amusing to communicate. Of course it was not in the nature of things that I should learn to know him here as his friends and neighbors at home knew him. I can only speak of him as he impressed himself upon me from time to time as I saw him here. He was evidently a gentleman of well-marked traits of character. He had shrewdness and energy in an eminent degree. He too was self-possessed and self-reliant. These qualities all combined made him at once a valuable friend and a dangerous antagonist. He impressed me too as a man of a remarkably good memory, with a great aptitude for details in all the practical affairs of life. His cast of mind, too, was eminently practical. He had no taste for mere theories. With him the great question seemed to be what was it best to do under the circumstances by which he was surrounded, and when that was solved he hesitated no longer. There are some phases of political life, too, to which he seemed peculiarly adapted. He was especially observant as to the political maneuverings of the politicians of all parties. In such matters he was usually remarkably well-informed. To him I have often been indebted for my first information as to current political events which were not yet publicly known.

I will not, however, Mr. Speaker, attempt an analysis of the character of the deceased, nor will I dwell upon any of the incidents of his official life. These have already been sufficiently referred to by others. Sir, it was but the other day—perhaps not a week before his death—that on my way to the Capitol I fell in with him on the Avenue, and we came on the rest of the way together. In our rather desultory conversation which ensued I referred to the fact that he would not be with us in the next Congress, and inquired of him how he felt about returning to private life again. He responded with seeming cheerfulness, that he was quite willing to quit Congress for a while, and possibly forever. Referring to his age, he said it was getting time he would settle down a little more quietly than he had been for many years past. "But," said he, "I have plenty to do at home in looking after my business; besides, political matters have not been going right for some time in Pennsylvania, and I will then have more time to help straighten things up there." Continuing, he further remarked: "I am good for several years' hard work yet, and I am not going to give up politics entirely if I do quit Congress."

He was then, Mr. Speaker, apparently as full of life and of plans for the future as any of us here to-day, and as totally unconscious that the relentless hand of death was already stretched out to receive him. You can judge then of my surprise, sir, of the shock which it imparted, when on the wings of the lightning the news came to us of his death only a few days later. No man of all my acquaintances seemed to have a fairer hold on life for a few years to come than he. Yet without a note of warning he has been stricken down. From the dust he came, and to the earth he has returned. As but yesterday he was a part of that living, breathing, moving, restless energy we call human life, to-day all that remains of him to us is as cold, as inert. and as lifeless as the clay in which he rests.

What a fearful admonition of the uncertainty of human life! How thin the drapery which separates us from eternity! And yet we go on planning, scheming, projecting, as if we had a perpetual lease of life, as if the "eternal years of God" were ours.

Mr. Speaker, a strong man has fallen, another chair is vacant in this Hall, another familiar face has disappeared from among us forever. And we, his survivors, can but bow in reverence to that divine will which has thus decreed the time and manner of his death. I also concur in seconding the resolutions which have been offered.

REMARKS OF MR. MAYNARD, OF TENNESSEE.

The request by the friends of the deceased to take a part in these obituary ceremonies cannot be denied. It is the common desire of us all, when in the hour of bereavement we appeal to our fellow-men. be they strangers or friends, in the language of the patriarch, to help

2

us bury our dead out of our sight. and must not be unheeded. The feeling is as old as death and as wide as humanity. All unite with one accord in granting immunity to the grave. The forms of the departed are gently laid away; their memory is tenderly cherished. No man of sensibility will vex the sepulcher; and the injunction to speak well of the dead, or not at all, is a precept which antedates Christianity. Here all rivalries cease, all resentments are extinguished, all contentions are hushed. The brotherhood of mortality meet at the common gateway, wide and ever open, through which all, soon or late, are destined to pass. Thither our bewildered footsteps, be they swift or be they slow, are constantly tending. The soul is awed in the presence of its own appointed doom. *In tempore sum, de tempore loquor, at nescio quid sit tempus*, is the confession of St. Augustine; and he might have made it, in phrase slightly changed, of the kindred mysteries, life, death, and eternity, as well as of time. Time is so identified with life, and death with eternity, that in speaking of the dead we unconsciously transcend the rules of judgment applied to the living, and, passing by the infirmities incident to the present sphere, dwell with satisfaction and comfort upon the more solid and enduring qualities which seem appropriate to the other.

It is now almost fourteen years since I first met the deceased as a member of this House. Though not at that time politically associated, our relations from the first were kind, soon friendly, never intimate. At that day he was one of the most active and zealous, and I think the most effective, opponents of Mr. Buchanan's administration from his own State. Not a man of education or culture, as these terms are usually understood, nor yet an orator, according to the canons of the schools, he was what neither oratory nor culture nor education can make; he was a worker, tireless and fearless. He had no confidence in the Administration, and believed it to be very corrupt; and therefore moved in the House for a committee to investigate its action. The results were embodied in an elaborate report, accompanied by voluminous testimony, which produced a deep and painful impression upon the public mind. Justice, I am inclined to think, both to him and to Mr. Buchanan, would require the revision of the report by the light of subsequent events. The Administration was so complicated with the incipient rebellion, the same characters being conspicuous in both, Cabinet officers and rebel leaders, that it requires great discrimination to decide for what of its acts it was responsible and as to what it was merely unfortunate. The time has not yet arrived, and if it had this is not the occasion, to pursue the inquiry. And the suggestion is thrown out merely for the purpose of the further remark that had Mr. Covode lived no one would have been more ready than he to correct any injustice into which he might have been unwittingly betrayed. Of conscious injustice, of intended wrong, however bitter the provocation, I think he was incapable.

During the war, even while not in public life, he gave to the Government an earnest and efficient support. Like so many others of the prominent men of that day, he offered his own son a sacrifice upon the altar of the country; and we have all seen his eyes grow dim with natural tears when recalling the memory of the gallant boy. He became satisfied very early in the contest that we were virtually resisting the power of Great Britain, and anticipated an open declaration of hostilities with that government. Though pained beyond measure to find an enemy where he thought we had a right to expect a friend, he did not hesitate about accepting the issue—doubtful and destructive as it certainly appeared. He was ready to stake all he had upon it and to abide the fate of his country. As might be supposed, he sympathized actively with the soldiers in the field; often visiting them in camp and using great diligence in providing for their wants, and in correcting the many irregularities incident to the volunteer service, especially in the earlier years, before either officers or men had become trained to the art of war and inured to its hardships.

His subsequent public career is too recent and too familiar for detail. Certain cardinal principles of action have regulated his course in our legislation. He believed that the issues of the war should be finally settled so as not to be reopened for the annoyance and consternation of future times; that the settlement should be confirmed by fair and reasonable guarantees; that the colored race, emancipated during the war, and as a war measure, should have their freedom secured beyond peradventure as a real, substantial boon, and not as an illusory thing; and, in short, that no man of any race or residence should ever have reason to regret that he had actively espoused the cause of the Union.

His politics were peculiarly of the old Whig school. The doctrines embodied with special clearness by Mr. Clay, in what he denominated the American system, as opposed to the British system, he deemed identified with the highest development and the largest prosperity of this continent. Nor was he a mere theorist. For many years I have understood he was actively engaged in different branches of. productive industry, and with marked success. His record upon all questions connected with the material interests of the people will be found in harmony with these views.

I have intimated that he was not a scholar. As implying a knowledge of books, beyond the Book of books, of which he was a diligent student and a firm believer, the remark is just. But in a wider and larger sense he was not untaught. He had a fair knowledge of men and of things. Few could more wisely decide the ends to be accomplished or more judiciously select the means for their accomplishment.

What need that I add a single word touching the character of this self-poised and self-reliant man? For us who knew him, none. His kind and genial humor, his unfailing good nature, his relish for merriment, and his almost boyish fondness for the joyous and playful, endeared him to us all as a friend to be loved and an opponent not to be hated. And when the tidings came so sudden, so shocking to us who as it seemed but the day before had greeted him in the House, that without warning he had been stricken down, each felt that his own circle had been invaded and one of its most agreeable members taken away.

His domestic relations, I have reason to say, were unusually affectionate and tender; and the resolution of condolence with the bereaved family, customary on similar occasions, will in this instance carry a peculiar significance.

His moral character, as distinguished from his social and domestic character, has been summed up by the popular voice in the single epithet, "Honest John Covode." Such contemporary estimates of character are seldom wrong and rarely reversed. And I feel sure of being sustained in ascribing to him the attributes of one of the best-drawn characters of antiquity:

"When the ear heard me, then it blessed me; and when the eye saw me, it gave witness to me: Because I delivered the poor that cried, and the fatherless, and him that had none to help him. The blessing of him that was ready to perish came upon me; and I caused the widow's heart to sing for joy. I was eyes to the blind, and feet was I to the lame. I was a father to the poor: and the cause which I knew not I searched out. And I brake the jaws of the wicked, and plucked the spoil out of his teeth. Unto me men gave ear, and waited, and kept silence at my counsel. After my words, they spake not again."

REMARKS OF MR. GETZ, OF PENNSYLVANIA.

Mr. Speaker: "I come to bury Cæsar, not to praise him." To speak truth of the dead, though an ungracious duty, is honester far than to pronounce the fulsome eulogy which makes an immaculate saint of him who while he lived frankly confessed himself a sinner. As a party man Mr. Covode was extreme, uncompromising, and, his opponents thought, unscrupulous. With him politics meant warfare, and he that was not with him was against him, and treated as an enemy to whom no quarter was to be granted. I knew him long in the political affairs of our State, and so radically did we differ upon all the questions that have divided parties during the past twenty years that I cannot remember a single instance in which we were in accord. It was only when I became associated with him in Congress that my personal acquaintance with him commenced, and that the opportunity was afforded me of learning that he whom I had always looked upon as an implacable political adversary possessed traits of character that made him susceptible to the warmest personal friendship.

Of his public career the colleagues who acted with him have spoken, and with commendation. Of his private life as a man and a citizen I feel free to say a few words, because I can say them in honor to his memory. With no advantages of early education, and with none of the adventitious aids to advancement that many of his compeers enjoyed in their youth, he achieved both fortune and fame by his own inherent force of character. Untiring industry, indomitable energy, frugality without parsimony, an intellect quick to apprehend, and a judgment remarkably acute to apply the knowledge he acquired in his intercourse with men, were the elements that combined to make his life, in a worldly point of view, a success. The secret of his popularity at home consisted in the fact that after he had risen to affluence and attained to honorable public station, he did not, as many have done under similar circumstances, turn his back upon the scene of his early and humble toil and take up his abode amid the splendors of fashionable life, where his wealth and position would have drawn toward him that society which is so much coveted by man's vain ambition, but remained at the old secluded homestead, on the romantic but rugged and wild mountains of Westmoreland, and employed his time and means in developing and improving not only his immediate neighborhood, but the whole of Western Pennsylvania.

John Covode had his faults, as who of us has not? But whatever may be recorded against him in the great book of God's remembrance, there will also be entered to his credit many an act of kindness, many a generous deed, many a work of charity, many a token of pure friendship. His death was sudden; so sudden and startling that when the intelligence first reached this city it was hardly credited. It was a surprise to all; and may I not say that none who knew him heard it confirmed without a pang of sorrow? Like the great statesman of Kentucky, no man had warmer friends and none more bitter enemies. Now that he has gone to "the undiscovered country from whose bourn no traveler returns," the latter may properly imitate the magnanimity of Henry Clay, who, when it was expected that he would rejoice at the death of his life-long foe, bowed his head in sorrow and feelingly exclaimed, "When God lays his hand upon my enemy I take mine off."

For myself, burying all partisan animosity in the grave that has but lately closed over John Covode's remains, I shall henceforth bear him in the same kindly remembrance that I know he would have borne for me had death summoned me hence before him.

REMARKS OF MR. HALDEMAN, OF PENNSYLVANIA.

' Mr. SPEAKER: Those of us from Pennsylvania who have been somewhat engaged in public affairs have long known John Covode by general repute; and in the brief period during which I was personally acquainted with him I found him to correspond to the general conception I had previously formed. He had a kind heart, but an unyielding will. With marked intellectual and physical energy, the circumstances of his life were such as to develop all the strong elements of his character. The substratum of John Covode was true grit; the elements of his nature were granitic. Under any circumstances and in any of the spheres of life he would have been successful. But it was his good fortune to early feel that he was dependent on his own efforts and his unaided energies. Life was for him a battle, and in that battle he emerged from each successful struggle with a more clearly defined and more self-reliant character. The granite of his character was exposed to the blows of fortune; but each blow was like the sculptor's chisel, developing more clearly the well-defined lineaments and form and mind and heart of John Covode—the *man*—whom we all so familiarly knew. Adversity is necessary to the development of true manhood. Nations and individuals who are possessed of inherent vigor and strength emerge from great trials more complete and admirable.

Mr. Covode was not educated as the schools understand education. The son of a "redemptioner," and thrown chiefly upon his own resources, he obtained a better education and more complete development from victorious contact with the world than he who, born to ease and with all the facilities of technical education, emerges from the university with the idea that his education is ended; when truly he has merely acquired the educational tools with which he is to work out such fortune and accomplish such duty as Heaven sets him to do. The man who, like a Gladstone or a Disraeli, is born to comparative fortune and is crammed with all the learning of the schools, who has tasted of the delights of study and mental acquisition, who has luxuriated amid philosophical and scientific investigation, who has been tempted to pass his life in the serene enjoyment of his taste for art and science and research, far removed from the deceptions and trials and disappointments and uncongenial associations of public life, such a man who yet wrests himself away from laborious yet delightful days, to become a leader of men and take active part in the battle of life, deserves perhaps as much credit as one who, like Mr. Covode, is compelled to strive, and striving, win the prize. The one rises superior to his crushing mass of knowledge, whether profitable or unprofitable; he becomes the master of his acquirements, and is not mastered by them, as is too often the case. He shows his true grit by overcoming the natural tendency to ease and luxury, and bravely assumes his share of the burden of those who believe that each of us owe our best endeavors to the amelioration of the nation's and the race's condition. The other is so fortunate as to feel the constant goad—to be developed by necessity and adversity, but which he, too, overcomes. Each plays well his part, each fulfills the duties Providence has set him to do, and thereby gains true honor and esteem. Success is in the man, in the unyielding determination to overcome obstacles, whether those obstacles arise out of comfort and luxury, or out of adversity and want.

Each of these typical men would probably succeed in either sphere. But it is the great merit of our institutions and civil polity that eminent success is here possible and facilitated for nature's strong men, no matter whether fortuitously placed high or low, with or without the so-called advantages of fortune. Therefore, John

Covode's career is eminently typical. Such lives as his are the vindication and the glory of the Republic. They are numerous; they are on all sides of us. They point the true moral of free government, which is founded to cultivate and develop individual man in all those talents and gifts and yearnings which he has received from nature and nature's God; to give full scope for the exercise of his faculties and secure to him his just share of reward.

Mr. PRESIDENT: Again, and for the third time during this short session, are we reminded that the robes of office will not ward away the shafts of death. Another of our colleagues has fallen, and we lay aside our labors for a few brief moments to pay a tribute to his memory.

Hon. John Covode, late Representative of the twenty-first congressional district of Pennsylvania, died at Harrisburg, on the 11th of January. He had left this city a few days previous, proceeded to his home, and with his wife went to Philadelphia, and made arrangements to place two of his younger children at school. Intending to resume his duties in the House, he started to return by way of Harrisburg. There, in his usual robust health, he retired to rest for a few hours before leaving for Washington. Attacked by acute pain in the region of the heart, he awoke, called his wife, and had medical aid summoned. Remedies were administered, but within an hour he died.

John Covode was born in Westmoreland County, Pennsylvania, on the 17th of March, 1808. His father was of Dutch and his mother of Quaker descent. An untarnished name was the only heritage they had to leave their son. His facilities for acquiring an education were very limited. His after life, however, demonstrated that his will would yield to no difficulties which perseverance could overcome; that obstacles in his path gave birth to the resolve that he would surmount them.

When quite young he left his home and traveled on foot to the State of New York, wishing to acquire a knowledge of some branch of manufacturing industry. He selected the fulling business, correctly calculating that one of the necessities of his native district could be supplied by the introduction of a fulling mill. He learned

the trade, returned and established what was known for years as
Covode's woolen factory. Although small, when compared with the
huge enterprises of the present day, it supplied the wants of the neighborhood. He was an honest, industrious, business man, and gained
the confidence of all who knew him. Growing in knowledge and
experience, seizing the opportunities which the advance of improvements offered, he employed his energies beyond the limits of his own
vicinity, and made the welfare of other sections of the State the object
of his solicitude.

Pennsylvania had commenced, in 1826, an extensive system of
internal improvements, and many who feared the burden of public
debt necessary to their completion shrunk back from the undertaking.
Men of nerve and courage were needed for that time. Of that class
was Mr. Covode. Confident in the value of the boundless but
undeveloped resources of the great Commonwealth, he gave an
ardent support to all measures for the commencement, prosecution,
and completion of her canals and railroads. When these furnished
insufficient facilities for trade and travel he again gave his efficient
aid. He was one of the original friends of the company incor-
porated in 1846 to construct a railroad from east to west through
the central portion of the State, and did much to secure its success.

When these improvements by State and company enterprise were
completed he was among the first to originate schemes for utilizing
them. He became a transporter on the canal, and, while the
railroad was in progress, organized companies to develop the coal-
fields in Western Pennsylvania, which it made accessible. In all
these he was a ruling and an active spirit, and, aided to a great
extent by his prudent management, they have prospered largely and
rewarded his sagacity and labors with abundant success. His
perseverance, foresight, self-confidence, hopefulness, and honesty of
purpose had all been exercised in behalf of his immediate neighborhood, county, and State, but it was not until he entered upon his
political career that those qualities became so conspicuous as to
attract the attention of the country. Before his election to Congress
in 1854 he had been a candidate for the State senate in the district

composed of the counties of Westmoreland and Somerset. Defeated by a very small majority, the canvass demonstrated his hold upon the confidence of the people. His party was in the minority, but many opposed to him politically waived their adherence to party rule, casting their votes for him as the Whig candidate.

In 1854 Mr. Covode was, for the first time, a candidate for Congress in the then nineteenth congressional district of Pennsylvania, and was elected. He was re-elected in 1856, 1858, and 1860. In the legislation immediately preceding the attempted secession of the Southern States, he was a prominent and courageous actor in resisting the encroachments of conspirators against the Union, and in exposing the schemes for the extension of slavery. In opposing the efforts to force the institution upon Kansas, he battled with all his energy, and became conspicuous for his industry and labors as chairman of a committee to investigate the influences by which this result was sought to be accomplished.

In the Thirty-sixth Congress, that immediately preceding the election of Mr. Lincoln to the Presidency, he contributed largely in preparing the public mind for a change in the policy on which the National Government had been administered. When that change came and secession followed, Mr. Covode stood unflinchingly by the flag of his country. He was not a man of soft words and persuasive speech. The time had come when it was to be decided by the arbitrament of the sword, whether the Union should be preserved or be severed into fragments. He advocated the strengthening of the arm of the Government to meet the attack of its enemies. His patriotic exhortations, though not couched in the flowery language of the rhetorician, were such as carried conviction to the minds of the people, and roused them to a sense of the impending dangers.

From the inauguration of the rebellion until the 4th day of March, 1863, when Mr. Covode voluntarily retired from Congress, after having served four successive terms, he was recognized as the enthusiastic defender of his country's weal and safety, serving during that time with vigor as a member of the Joint Committee on the Conduct of the War. But he gave even stronger proof of his loyal devotion than by his individual efforts as a member of Congress. He gave to his country three of his sons to do battle in the field, one of whom, Colonel George Covode, was killed in battle near Richmond; another returned from the prison-house at Andersonville, broken in health, and now remains a lingering evidence of the cruelty there inflicted upon the unfortunate Union prisoners; a third completed his term of enlistment and was honorably discharged.

At the close of the Thirty-seventh Congress Mr. Covode retired temporarily from public life. Though in no official position, he did not remain an inactive spectator of the continued struggle of parties. In 1862 and in 1864 his district was carried by the Democrats. To effect a change in the representation he again became a candidate in 1866. His personal and political popularity, backed by his great energy, secured an election. In 1868 he was again chosen to represent his district in the House of Representatives, and in 1869 he conducted the political campaign as chairman of the Republican State central committee. Such is a brief sketch of the leading incidents of his business and public life, and they, to a great extent, indicate his character.

He was not a man of learning; he was a man of intellect. It was not that cultivated intellect which often leads men to be mere thinkers, whose thoughts end in dreams and are sometimes afterward caught up and made practical by the earnest workers of the world. His was that busy, practical brain which made him a man of action, a type of the untiring working men who are making their mark upon this active century, who study their fellow-men more than books, and who are indispensable to the earnest thinkers of the age. Earnest thinkers and earnest workers need each other. Earnest thought is earnest work in one sense, but not in all senses. The earnest thought of the commander who plans a campaign or maps out a battle-field may be earnest work for him; but it is not that kind of earnest work which carries forts and routs opposing armies. The men who do this kind of earnest work should live in history, as well as those who plan it and direct it to be done.

I saw recently a large painting of the battle of Gettysburg,

ordered by the State of Pennsylvania. It represents the pinch of
the fight—the repulse of Pickett's charge. Its central figure is a
private Union soldier—tall, muscular, with all the energy of determined action apparent in every feature and in every limb—with a
musket clenched frantically in his hands, and drawn to strike an
assailant.   He seems to be the real leader of all who are behind him.
The commanding generals are in the dim distance.   I thought, as I
looked upon it, that the men of action are, in our day, coming to
the front.

Such a man was John Covode.   His speeches do not fill many
columns of the Globe.   His actions have influenced events which will
employ the pens of many historians; and if the thoughts and the
reasonings, during our years of trial, of such men as Stevens and
Fessenden among the dead, of others whom I may not in good
taste here name among the living, shall afford food for the students
who shall come after us, the deeds of John Covode, as they stand
upon the same record, in the same years, will command the gratitude
of the patriot's heart.   In the word-painting of history his name will
not be left out.   ·

He was bold, energetic, self-reliant, and persevering.   He investi-
gated for himself, he decided for himself, and, when he decided, the
next step was to act.   Some friends were proposing to him to
examine into the practicability of a railroad up the valley of the
Platte, and wished to submit the opinion of an engineer.   "Let us
go and see for ourselves," said Mr. Covode, and he went, taking
some of his friends with him.   His own examination decided his
course upon that question.

But although energetic and self-reliant, he was neither repellant
nor selfish.   Warm as a partisan, he was genial and generous in
social life and as a personal friend.   I will not say of him that he
had no enemies; for if I did it would imply, in my belief, that he
had failed in some of life's duties.   He had the nerve to do right as
he saw the right; and the man who does that, either in private or
public life, will have enemies.

He was the friend and trusted counselor of the poor and dependent.

Having himself come up from the vale of poverty, he sympathized with the sorrows of those in want. He certainly had never read, in the original, Dido's address to Æneas, and it may be he could not have quoted Dryden's translation of her sentiment—

"I learn to pity woes so like my own,"

but he did what was better than scanning Latin or quoting English verse. When the needy came to him he did not exhaust his sympathy for the poor in sentiment for their class. He ministered to the needy man or woman before him, asking aid.

I cannot refrain from expressing here the thoughts that were prompted by the scene at his funeral, which I attended, upon the invitation of the committee appointed by the House. His residence was in a deep and narrow valley. As we neared it, Hendricks Creek, named by the ancestors of Senator Hendricks, came in sight, wending its way along the foot of a high hill. Steep hills were on every side of us, and it seemed that there was no outlet for the struggling stream. But it finds its way after many windings, and, passing through the tributaries of the Alleghany, flows on to the Gulf, mingling its waters with that stream which, by its genial warmth, breaks up the frozen regions of the North. Was it this surrounding that impelled John Covode to action? Did he look out over the high hills which, on every side, shut him from the busy world beyond, and resolve that he, too, with his strong German common sense, keeping him ever on the plane of right; with his warm Quaker heart throbbing in unison with the aspirations of the oppressed for freedom and the equal rights of man, would go out and cast his influence into that great gulf stream of enlightened and advancing public sentiment, which was breaking up the polar sea of human bondage? This he had done, and he had lived to see liberty proclaimed "through all the land, to all the inhabitants thereof."

But his race was run; and there he was dead, his sorrowing friends and stricken wife and children, his sympathizing neighbors, all shocked by the suddenness and severity of the affliction. The loss sustained by that bereaved family is one which no earthly hand can temper, no human sympathy can lessen. The loss sustained by the community in which he lived was attested by the presence of the people of all ranks and conditions of life, to pay the last tribute of respect to his memory. High and low, rich and poor, were there. On foot, on horseback, in the road wagon, in the carriage, in every way that men and women could travel, did the long funeral procession wend its way to the little village church-yard, in the county of his birth, to lay him in his last resting-place, by the side of his gallant son, and surrounded by the tablets which tell the "short and simple annals of the poor."

If a man's life has not impressed his fellow-men, his funeral will not. But his funeral may tell how his life has impressed them; and, standing there, no man could doubt the sincerity of the sorrow which his death had occasioned among those who knew him best. A bad man could not be so mourned. Taken as he was, without warning, away from the busy scenes of life's activities, when looking forward to new and important enterprises, his death admonishes us who are engaged, as he was, in public cares and duties, of the uncertainty of life and of the value of our time; that we should

> "Part with it as with money, sparing; pay
> No moment but in purchase of its worth;
> And what its worth, ask death-beds; they can tell."

Mr. President, I offer the following resolutions:

Resolved, That the Senate has received with deep sensibility the announcement of the death of the late Hon. John Covode, late a member of the House of Representatives from the State of Pennsylvania.

Resolved, That as a mark of respect for the memory of Mr. Covode, the members of the Senate will wear the usual badge of mourning for thirty days.

Resolved, That as a further mark of respect for the memory of the deceased, the Senate do now adjourn.

REMARKS OF MR. SUMNER, OF MASSACHUSETTS.

Mr. PRESIDENT: I venture to interpose a brief word of sincere homage to the late John Covode. I call him John Covode, for so I heard him called always. Others are known by some title of honor or office, but he was known only by the simple name he bore. This familiar designation harmonized with his unassuming life and character.

During his long service in Congress I was in the Senate, so that I have been his contemporary. And now that he has gone before me I owe my testimony to the simplicity, integrity, and patriotism of his public life. Always simple, always honest, always patriotic, he leaves a name which must be preserved in the history of Congress. In the long list of its members he will stand forth with an individuality not to be forgotten. How constantly and indefatigably he toiled the records of the other House declare. He was a doer rather than a speaker; but is not doing more than speech, unless in those rare cases where a speech is an act? But his speech had a plainness which was not without effect, especially before the people, where the facts and figures which he presented with honest voice were eloquent.

The rebellion found this faithful Representative in his place, and from the first moment to the last he gave to its suppression time, inexhaustible energy, and that infinite treasure, the life of a son. He was for the most vigorous measures, whether in the field or in statesmanship. Slavery had no sanctity for him, and he insisted upon striking it. In the same spirit, when the rebellion was suppressed, he insisted always upon those Equal Rights for All, without which the Declaration of Independence is an unperformed promise, and our nation a political bankrupt. In all these things he showed character and became a practical leader. There is heroism elsewhere than on fields of battle, and he displayed it. He was a civic hero. And here the bitterness which he encountered was the tribute to his virtue.

In doing honor to this much-deserving servant, I cannot err if I add that nobody had more at heart the welfare of the Republican party, with which, in his judgment, were associated the best interests of the nation. He felt that, giving to his party, he gave to his country and to mankind. His strong sense and the completeness of his devotion to party made him strenuous always for those commanding principles by which humanity is advanced. Therefore was he for the unity of the party, that it might be directed with all its force for the good cause. Therefore was he against outside and disturbing questions, calculated to distract and divide. He saw the wrong they did to the party, and, in the relation of cause and effect, to the country. And here that frankness, which was part of his nature, became a power. He was always frank, whether with the people, with Congress, or with the President. I cannot forget his frankness with Abraham Lincoln, who, you know, liked frankness. On more than one occasion with this good President his frankness conquered. Honorable as was such a victory to the simple Representative, it was more honorable to the President.

His honest indignation at wrong was doubtless quickened by the blood which coursed in his veins and the story which it constantly whispered. He was descended from one of those "redemptioners" or indented servants transported to Pennsylvania in the middle of the last century, being a species of white slaves, among whom was one of the signers of the Declaration of Independence. The eminence which John Covode reached attests the hospitality of our institutions and shows how character triumphs over difficulties. With nothing but a common education, he improved his condition, gained riches, enlarged his mind with wisdom, and won the confidence of his fellow-citizens, until he became an example.

The death of such a citizen makes a void, but it leaves behind a life which in itself is a monument.

REMARKS OF MR. SHERMAN, OF OHIO.

Mr. PRESIDENT: Again we are called upon to share in the last sad ceremonies on the occasion of the death of one of our old associates. Mr. Covode entered upon his public life in the Thirty-fourth Congress. He was elected a member of Congress in the fall of 1854, when for the first time the anti-slavery sentiment of the Northern States, aroused by the Kansas-Nebraska bill, contested for supremacy in the administration of the National Government. The commencement of this struggle dates back to the origin of the Government, and indeed was inherent in the nature of the human mind. The ideas that ruled a society where a great portion of the people were slaves, and the ideas that controlled a people all free, were of necessity in a state of chronic war. That they did not sooner come in armed conflict is the highest evidence of the forbearance, obedience, and respect for law that is the distinguishing trait of our race. But when the geographical barriers erected by our fathers had been broken down in the interest of slavery the conflict became inevitable. The mass of our people, with a keen perception of the nature of the conflict, arrayed themselves into parties distinctively founded upon these antagonistic ideas. Old party divisions melted away; other issues were subordinated or postponed; and in the House of Representatives of the Thirty-fourth Congress the conflict commenced which in the end destroyed slavery and left us in all the States with institutions in harmony with republican liberty.

Mr. Covode, though a Whig in politics, was elected in a Democratic district; and I met him for the first time in December, 1855. in the long struggle that followed over the organization of the House. From that time until his death my acquaintance with him was intimate. He took an active but peculiar part in all the political contests of the time. And now, sir, in reviewing his life, for the purpose of joining in this tribute to his memory, I can truthfully say that I knew no one in public life who was a truer friend, more faithful to his convictions of duty, less influenced by bitterness and malignity, and who was less changed by his long political service from the plain John Covode of our early acquaintance. It so happened that I once visited his district and sought the secret of his continued popularity at his home, where there had been many political changes. He had been engaged extensively in many

branches of business, had been very successful, had accumulated a
large fortune, from a laboring-man had become the employer of
thousands of laborers, had held high official position; and yet in
all these changes had continued the same plain-hearted, genial,
kind, and accessible John Covode.

His success did not excite envy, and even among his political
adversaries, though he was a very decided partisan, there was no
bitterness. With his political associates in the House of Representatives he was popular and influential, never contesting the higher
honors of political strife or leading in debate; yet his good will and
good offices were eagerly sought by others, and when given were
always sincere and useful. I do not think any one can truly say
he was ever misled or deceived by Mr. Covode. His sagacity in
political matters was intuitive. He felt and knew the popular pulse,
because he mingled with and knew the people as well as any man
in public life. In his popular addresses he was far more successful
than learned and polished lawyers who depended upon studied
preparation. His speeches were earnest, direct, and good-humored,
and did not lose their force though his grammar was not always
correct and his ideas were clothed in homely phrase. Mr. Covode
was one of the many who under our free institutions, without advantage of education, but with native talents, great industry, and
energy, filled the measure of a successful life.

He did great good in developing the resources of his State; he
was true to his political convictions; he was firm in his friendships;
he was a good husband and father; and now, sir, that he is suddenly
taken from us by death, treading a little time before us the dim,
gloomy, impenetrable paths of future life, we, his old associates, can
recall his memory with kindness, respect, and affection. When we
reflect how few of the members of the Thirty-fourth Congress still
fill their places in these Halls, and how many, both of our friends
and adversaries, are now dead—falling here and there in the changing
phases of life without creating a ripple in the great current of events—
we feel the insignificance of any one human life, however proudly
and prominently it may be for a moment in the public eye. All that

we can do is to contribute a little, and but a little, to the general progress of our country; and we must be content if, when our eulogies are pronounced, our survivors may say of us what has been truly said to-day of John Covode.

REMARKS OF MR. CAMERON, OF PENNSYLVANIA.

Mr. President: Leaving a particular statement and analysis of the life of Mr. Covode to gentlemen more intimate with it than I am, I design saying a few words of him and his career which I hope will impress the youth of the country. In him we have a bright illustration of what may be attained under a political system which invites every kind of ability to its service, which welcomes every description of talent, and excludes none from the responsibilities and honors of public life.

Mr. Covode encountered the difficulties which his humble extraction and poverty placed in his way with the steady courage of the race whose blood flowed in his veins. His father was one of those whose passage was paid from the Low Countries by service of redemption after his arrival on our shore. In early times the farmers and small manufacturers of Pennsylvania, true to the traditions of our State, procured this class of laborers in preference to slaves. That they were wise in this choice it is not now, happily, necessary to argue. But if proof were demanded it may be found in the beautiful valleys now possessed by the descendants of these imported laborers, by their high culture, by their thrift, and by the exalted honor which marks all their dealings. And it is worthy of honorable mention, in passing, that there is not one single instance in which these patient, honest people failed to carry out to the uttermost, and in perfect good faith, the contract by which they were enabled to come to a land of plenty.

However much of honor and fame John Covode may have earned by his public services, he holds a higher place in my esteem for the true courage he possessed. I never honored him more than when,

in a speech in Philadelphia not long ago, he boldly proclaimed what
other and weaker men would have labored to suppress, and an-
nounced as a reason for his hostility to every species of human bondage the fact that his father had been sold as a "redemptionist" near
the very spot where he was then speaking to thousands on matters of
high importance; standing up an acknowledged leader in a land
famous for the number and abilities of its leading men and the aver-
age intelligence of its people.

This German element in Pennsylvania, of which Mr. Covode was
an excellent type, found itself, from very early times, in sharp rivalry
with another race with which no ordinary qualities could maintain a
successful struggle. The bold and enterprising Scotch-Irish and
Scotch were already there. While these people were furnishing the
pioneers for our constantly advancing frontier, they yet left behind
them a strong force to dispute with all comers the possession of the
land their courage had conquered from the savage and the wilder-
ness. These and the Swedes were mainly the purchasers of the laborers who were brought from Europe, and were the owners of much of
the soil. But scarcely a generation had passed away before the hired
servants began to buy their masters' lands, to marry their masters'
daughters, and to make good their claim to full equality with those
whose bondmen they had been. For a time the Scoth-Irish made a
sturdy stand for that supremacy and superiority which seem to be
their peculiar inheritance, place them where you may. At length the
thrift, the superior patience, and the perseverance of the German
blood prevailed. They bought, and still possess, the old homesteads,
and have furnished us with an array of distinguished men of whom
every citizen of our State is justly proud; while their rivals, true to
their character for progress and enterprise, spread westward to our
borders. There they took firm root. And from that citadel of their
power they have furnished the picket-guard of civilization for the
continent. While the sons of the Germans from generation to generation inherited their fathers' lands, they continued in the simple pur-
suits of their ancestors. The Scotch-Irish, on the other hand, sent
their sons to colleges, and constantly asserted their claims to power

and direction; the result of which is that this race has furnished us with more Presidents than all others combined, and has put its indelible impress on the political institutions of our country.

There is nothing either new or striking in what I have said; and it may be considered as foreign to the object for which I arose. But to me it seemed necessary in considering the lesson of a useful man's life, and so germane to my purpose.

John Covode was the irreconcilable foe of slavery because, in the traditions of his family, that detestation was the outgrowth of experience, of bitter suffering, of unmerited reproach. He loved liberty as one to whom its beauty was a reality and not merely a sentiment. And so the same practical traits are to be seen all through his character. As one denied the blessings and advantages of education, he was an unflinching friend of free schools. As an American laborer, his life was spent in shielding American labor from the blight of foreign competition. As a Pennsylvanian, he loved the State which gave him birth and sepulcher to his fathers. As an American citizen, he loved the land where he and his kindred found refuge and honor. His was a sympathetic heart, and his hand was open. He alleviated the sorrows and afflictions of his neighbors with unstinted generosity. And the vast concourse of those that flocked to his funeral to pay honor to his remains is conclusive evidence of the high estimation in which he was held by those who knew him best.

And this, after all, is the touchstone of true popularity. The attendance of the great men of the nation who represented Congress at his burial; of the refined gentlemen, his associates in business and in humanitarian projects; of the eminent men who left everything to add their tribute of respect to the obsequies of their friend, was indeed honorable to them and just to his memory. But the simple, manly grief of his neighbors far outweighs all these, and casts an honor over his grave which all else was incapable of reflecting.

Confident that I have spoken but imperfectly of Mr. Covode's character, I yet feel that what I have said is not in vain. Some youth, struggling in obscurity against an adverse fortune, and beset with difficulties which appear at times insurmountable, will read of our dead colleague's struggle and victory, and take fresh courage. If even one such shall thereby emerge from his difficulties, and give to his country and his fellow-men the strong common sense and the acute understanding of another John Covode, my object will have been attained. And I cannot pay higher honor to the dead than to present his life as an example to the young men of our country, claiming, as I do, the liberty of age and experience to press this example on their attention, and pointing them to the struggles, the success, and the end of the life of our departed friend.

I second, sir, the resolutions offered by my colleague.

www.ingramcontent.com/pod-product-compliance
Lightning Source LLC
Chambersburg PA
CBHW021443090426
42739CB00009B/1610